INTERCESSORS ARISE

Book for Prayer and Intercession

Written by
DR. DWAN YVETTE JACKSON

ISBN 979-8-88862-918-5

This book provides accurate and authoritative information regarding the subject matter covered. This information is given to understand that neither the author nor LEEDS PRESS CORP is engaged in rendering legal or professional advice. The opinions expressed by the author are not necessarily those of LEEDS PRESS CORP

DEDICATION

I want to dedicate this book to my family. My husband and my children. I want to thank you for all your labor of love and your sacrifices to allow me to always be available for the body of Christ. I thank you for always being by my side for your love and your support. God will make sure that each of you are rewarded. I stand in agreement that all your heart's desires will come forth. We have been able to apply many of these types of prayers together and as I have grown you have also grown. I salute each of you. To my mom who is now in heaven thank you for allowing your legacy to live on in me and to be such an example to my life.

To my friend Overseer Solomon James who has been a great instrument in my life to bring the next level in prayer. Thank you for pushing me in prayer like never before. God bless you and your family.

To my Spiritual Dad, thank you for never giving up on me and continually pushing me to my fullest potential in Christ , Apostle Dr. Lloyd Benson Sr.

PREFACE
APOSTLE DR. DWAN JACKSON

My name is Dwan Jackson, and I was born and raised in Rochester, New York. As far back as I can remember I was regularly taken to church services. And at the tender age of five, I gave my life to Christ. I remember being the only child who was made to be in prayer services every Wednesday night with my mom and the much older people. However, the older I got, my mom would often say to me, "You're different. You can't do these things others your age is doing because you have a different assignment." I was in prayer for years until it became normal for me to pray about everything. My mom was an intercessor and she always prayed; it was a lifestyle for her. In every situation, she'd always say, "Let me see what God would want us to do". She taught me to pray. I never understood that until I got older, and it was then I realized I was called to be an intercessor and I learned what being an intercessor meant.

Prayer for me was a time to tell God all that I wanted and to understand and know that he was listening. As this journey continued God allowed me to travel to different countries to minister to people of all different backgrounds. I then realized we had not learned as much about prayer as we should have in our churches in the western world. I started exploring more in prayer having many encounters with God. I noticed God drew me closer to him and allowed me to see many things and to learn many things. I also begin to dig deeper in the word of God and realized there are so many things that can be learned about prayer. I learned that we could pray in so many ways and that there are prayers of supplication and prayers of intercession and prayers of travail among others. This book is to help people dive into praying in different styles and to share with others about the types of prayers.

I have led many prayers and have seen people be healed and set free from

bondages in their lives, to seeing people who have come out of critical situations in hospitals to those who have been given lengthy prison sentences and have that time miraculously reduced, to seeing those who have been oppressed being delivered. I also noticed in the time of my growth in my prayer ministry, not only were the gifts of God being developed even stronger, but God began to call me a prophet of God. I also learned there are many types of prophets and how they operate and after sitting under a prophet who was a man of God for many years I also was recognized as a prophet an began to walk heavily in the prophetic office. This is an office that has helped many people to hear the voice of God and to be directed by God through his servants who would be his mouthpiece. I developed that calling and walked in it not for many years and God allowed me to be birthed as a spirit bearer prophet and to function in that calling and also as a prophetic intercessor. I have now walked in both of these callings for over 20 years helping others in the body of Christ and those outside of the Christian world as well.

Prayer has changed my life. I went from praying 15 to 30 minutes a day, to learning how to labor for hours on hand before God, understanding how important this is. I understand that there are answers for everything in prayer. If we are willing to take the time to learn in prayer, we can get the answers we so desperately need. Are you willing to pay the price to get the answer you need from God for yourself or for others?

Prayer is not just a posture of asking God for things, it is communing with him and learning of his ways and what pleases him. The more we learn to do his will and to please him, he also grants rewards for us, and allows us to receive answers to things we desire to know. The word of God says that we are to ask any thing in his name, and it shall be given. That scripture has always fascinated me because I knew a lot of things that were asked for, but not given. The scripture can't be that simple even though it looks like it is. There must be a certain element that is missing. I understood that prayers are responded to under certain conditions. I realized that everything could happen if the conditions are right, and the principles are applied, and we do what is asked of us to do. Applying faith is another big part of prayer.

As I have gone on this journey, I continue to learn more and more about God through prayer and wanted to share some of what I have learned over the years. I believe this short book will empower you to get connected to God. It will spark something in you to want to not only learn more about prayer, but to become an intercessor. I really want to encourage you to go on this journey. I learned that prayer is not boring, prayer is not a chore, and it should be done out of obligation. Prayer is an active engagement with God and the spirit realm. Prayer does change things. Prayer has changed my life dramatically. I pray daily and I intercede on the behalf of others. Prayers can be declarations and prayers can be using your heavenly language. The bible teaches us that we ought to pray without ceasing (1 Thessalonians 5:17). This is a short yet very powerful scripture. I found that we need prayer and intercession, and God is raising up an army of people who will pray and intercede. I learned that intercession is the heartbeat of God. As I pray, I learn that prayer changes me. The bible speaks about how prayer begins to change our countenance when we pray. Even when Jesus prayed his life was changed and so was his countenance (Luke 9:28-29).

I want to invite someone to go on this life changing journey to begin to pray. Intercession is a calling. In Isaiah, the bible spoke about how God was looking for a man who would stand in the gap to change the situation and he found none. I am glad God called me to stand in the gap and to teach others about prayer. I have now birthed a school of ministry to teach others how to pray and to grow in their prayer life. I am also helping others with the knowledge of prayer and how to effectively pray. Please feel free to visit my YouTube channel for more information or feel free to register for my prayer classes, which is a 6- week course. You can register for the classes at freshmannaintl.ministries@gmail.com.

I know God has trained me over the last 30 years to pray and intercede. I believe this will help you as well to grow. One final thing I would like to share before you dive more into the book. I was praying and praying not understanding God was calling me into this new place. When I said yes it was like a weight lifted off of me and I realized I was right in the center of His will. I would always feel a burden for other people and wondered if they felt that same burden. I would feel others pain and I would wonder why anyone doesn't else feel this. I realized that God was birthing me to be an intercessor for the body of Christ. If this is, you then I believe this book will give you some clarity of the things that will help you to dive deeper into prayer.

I have learned there are many types of prayer such as corporate prayer, spiritual birthing in prayer, sack cloth and ashes prayer, binding and loosing prayers, apostolic prayers, prophetic prayers, model prayers, Davidic prayers, and the Lord's prayer. There are also sit-in prayers, prayer walks, mountain prayers, women's prayers, youth prayers, leadership prayers and many more. In this book you will see some of these things mentioned and I want to encourage you to follow up with me and to take my courses and I believe that you will be empowered and strengthened in prayer.

I learned how to chase the Lord. I learned how to fall in love with him. I learned I cannot do without prayer it is like your necessary food. We have to empty ourselves. Try to do 2 hours of prayer a day. You can break it down to do four 30-minute sessions or eight 15-minute sessions of prayer a day. Learn to release the blood of Jesus over yourself, this was a very important principle I learned, and I was able to apply. Understand that Prayer is the only answer to everything. Prayer has brought influence over my life and has brought me before kings and great leaders across the nations and has prospered my life in ways I could have never imagined. So, I pray you will become the next intercessor to arise.

Table of Contents

INTRODUCTION TO PRAYER 5
Objectives 5
Define Prayer 5
Key Verses 5
INTRODUCTION 7
How Prayer is Answered 7
Types Of Prayer 9
Worship and Praise 9
Praise and Worship Can Be With 10
Other Types of Prayers 11
PRAYER AND INTERCESSION 13
Instances of Intercessory Prayers 13
Intercessory Prayer Solicited 13
Intercessory Prayers Answered 14
INTERCESSORS 16
THE PRAYER LIFE OF JESUS 18
Jesus made prayer a priority 18
AUTHORITY AND POWER 20
Power of the Enemy 20
Power Over Sin 20
Power to Extend the Gospel 20
Binding and Loosing 21
A TEACHING ON WATCHES 23
References and Scriptures 27
Abraham Calling Upon the Name of The Lord 27
Crying unto God 28
Drawing near to God 29
Looking Up 33
Lifting up the Soul 33
Pouring out the heart 35

Pouring out the Soul 36

Crying to Heaven 38

Beseeching the Lord.. 41

Standing 44

Daniel was Praying on his Knees... 47

King Solomon, kneeling on his Knees with his Hands Spread up to Heaven

.... 50

INTRODUCTION TO PRAYER

Objectives

Upon completion of this chapter, you will be able to:

Define Prayer

- Explain how prayer is answered.
- Summarize the roles of prayer in the life of Jesus Christ.
- Identify the levels of prayer.
- Identify the different types of prayer.

Key Verses

Ask, and it shall be given you; seek, and ye shall find; knock, and it shall be opened unto you; for everyone that asketh recieveth; and he that seeketh findeth, and to him that knocketh it shall be opened (Matthew 7:7-8).

INTRODUCTION

This chapter introduces the subject of prayer. You will learn the definition of prayer and the importance Jesus placed on it. You will learn how prayer is answered and the different levels and types of prayer.

Calling upon the name of the Lord (Genesis 12:8)

Crying unto God (Psalms 27:7; 34:6)

Drawing near to God (Psalms 73:28; Hebrews 10:22)

Looking up (Psalms 5:3)

Lifting up the soul (Psalms 25:1)

Lifting up the heart (Lamentations 3:41)

Pouring out the heart (Psalms 62:8)

Pouring out the soul (1Samuel 1:15)

Crying to Heaven (2Chronicles 32:20)

Beseeching the Lord (Exodus 32:11)

How Prayer is Answered

The Bible reveals that prayer is answered.

Immediately at times : Isaiah 65:24; Daniel 9:21-23

Delayed at times : Luke 18:7

Different from our desires : 2Corinthians 12:8-9

Beyond our expectations : Jeremiah 33:3; Ephesians 3:2

Notes

Types Of Prayer

Paul calls for believers to pray always with "all prayer" (Ephesians 6:18). Another translation of the Bible reads "pray with every kind of prayer" (Goodspeed Translation). This refers to the various types of prayer which include:

Worship and Praise

You enter into God's presence with worship and praise: Enter into His gates with thanksgiving and into His courts with praise; be thankful unto Him and bless His Name (Psalms 100:4).

Worship is the giving of honor and devotion. Praise is thanksgiving and an expression of gratitude not only for what God has done but for who He is. You are to worship God in Spirit and in truth.

But the hour cometh, and now is, when the true worshipers shall worship the Father in Spirit and in truth; for the Father seeketh such to worship Him. God is a Spirit, and they that worship Him must worship Him in Spirit and in truth (John 4:23-24).

Worshiping God in truth means that you worship Him on the basis of what is revealed in the word of God. To worship Him in Spirit is to do so sincerely in the power of the Holy Spirit, from your inner- most being, putting Him first above all others. When you worship in Spirit, you allow the Holy Spirit to direct your worship. You do not use man-made formulas or rituals of worship. You don't just repeat chants or prayers with your mind somewhere else. Instead, you open up the innermost recesses of your heart and mind, and lift, praise and adoration to Him in your own words. Sometimes, the Holy Spirit will take over completely and you will begin to worship in the "other tongues" of your prayer language.

Praise and Worship Can Be With

Singing (Psalms 9:2, 11; 40:3; Mark 14:26)
Audible praise (Psalms 103:1)
Shouting (Psalms 47:1)
Lifting up of the hands (Psalms 63:4; 134:2; 1Timothy 2:8)
Clapping (Psalms 47:1)
Musical Instruments (Psalms 150:3-5)
Standing (2Chronicles 20:19)

Daniel was praying on his knees.
Kneeling is a type of prayer, 3 times a day.
Supplications (Daniel 6:10-11)

Solomon was praying and sending supplications.
Kneeling on his knees with his hands spread up to heaven.
(1Kings 8:54)

Standing in prayer
When you stand praying, forgive (Mark 11:25a)
A woman stood praying (1Samuel 1:26-27)

Jesus prays alone.
Praying alone is good as well (Luke 9:18)

Praying in locations
Praying in a certain place (Luke 11:1)

Other Types of Prayers

Intercession: The Spirit to pray through you and God to say what He wants (Rom. 8:26-27).

Supplication: a type of deep request and petitions made to God (Dan. 6:11; 1Kings 8:38-39) (found at least 58 times).

Travailing: A deep cry out of your spirit (Isa. 66:7-8, 42:14; Gal. 4:27) (found at least 46 times)

Weeping and Wailing: A deep cry in prayer out, it may be mourning from the spirit of the Lord or to bring out the sorrow of the situation before the Lord, a deep repentance (Joel 2:12-14, 17; Mal. 2:13) (found over 41 times).

Praying in the spirit: Praying in tongues and using the spirit to hear and get clarity and direction (Eph. 6:18; Jude 1:20; Acts 1:8, 14) (mentioned a few times in scripture).

Notes

____

____

____

____

____

____

____

____

____

____

____

____

____

____

____

____

PRAYER AND INTERCESSION

(Ezekiel 13:5; Ezekiel 22:30 and Acts 12:5-16)
GAP — a rent or opening in a wall (Ezek. 13:5; comp. Amos 4:3). The false prophets did not stand in the gap (Ezek. 22:30), i.e., they did nothing to stop the outbreak of wickedness.

Instances of Intercessory Prayers

Abraham on behalf of Sodom: Gen 18:23–32; on behalf of Abimelech: Gen 20:17- 18. Abraham's servant on behalf of his master: Gen 24:12. Jacob on behalf of his children: Gen 49. Moses on behalf of Pharaoh: Ex 8:12, 13, 30, 31; 9:33; 10:18, 19. Moses for Israel Num16:20-22; 21:7; Deut. 33:6–17; Psa. 106:23; for Miriam: Num. 12:13–15.

David for Israel: 2Samuel 24:17; Solomon for Israel: 1 Kings 8:29–53. Ezra for Israel: Ezra 9:5–15. Nehemiah on behalf of Judah and Je- rusalem: Neh. 1:4–9. Asaph for the church: Ps. 80:83. Korah for the church: Ps. 85:1–7. Jeremiah for Israel: Jer. 14:7–22. Amos for Israel: Amos 7:2–6. Disciples on behalf of Peter's wife's mother: Luke 4:38, 39 and Mark 9:17–27. Paul for the church: Acts 20:32.

Intercessory Prayer Solicited

By Pharaoh of Moses: Ex. 8:8, 28; 9:28; 10:17; 12:32; and by the Israelites: Num. 21:7. By Israel of Samuel: 1Sam. 12:19. By Jeroboam of a prophet: 1 Kin. 13:6. By Hezekiah of Isaiah: 2 Kings 19:1–4. By Zedekiah of Jeremiah: Jer. 37:3; and by Johanan: Jer. 42:1–6. By Dan- iel of Shadrach, Meshach and Abed-nego: Dan. 2:17-18. By Darius of the Jews: Ezra 6:10. By Simon Magus of Peter: Acts 8:24. By Paul of the churches: Rom. 15:30–32; 2 Cor. 1:11; Eph. 6:19, 20; 1

Thess.

5:25; 2 Thess. 3:1; Heb. 13:18.

Intercessory Prayers Answered

Moses on behalf of Pharaoh, for the plague of frogs to be abated: Ex. 8:12, 15; the plague of flies: Ex. 8:30–32; the plague of rain, thun-der, and hail: Ex. 9:27–35; plague of locusts: Ex. 10:16–20; plague of darkness: Ex. 10:21–23. Of Moses, for the Israelites during the battle with the Amalekites Amalekites: Ex. 17:11–14; after the Israelites had made the golden calf: Ex. 32:11–14, 31–34; Deut. 9:18-29; 10:10; Psa. 106:23.

After the complaining of the people: Ex. 33:15–17; when the fire of the Lord consumed the people: Num. 11:1, 2; when the people complained on account of the report of the spies: Num. 14:11–20; that the fiery serpents might be abated: Num. 21:4–9; that Miriam's leprosy might be healed: Num. 12:13; in behalf of Aaron, on account of his sin in making the golden calf: Deut. 9:20. Of Samuel, for deliverance from the oppressions of the Philistines: 1Sam. 7:5–14. The prophet of Israel, for the restoration of Jeroboam's withered hand: 1 Kings 13:1–6. Of Elijah, for the raising from the dead the son of the hospitable widow: 1 Kings 17:20–23. Of Elisha, for the raising from the dead the son of the Shunammite woman: 2 Kings 4:33–36. Of Isaiah, in behalf of Hezekiah and the people, to be delivered from Sennacherib: 2 Kings 19.

Notes

INTERCESSORS

An intercessor is one that makes requests or petitions to God on behalf of others. Intercessors are special people called by God to develop a relationship with Him to stand in the gap. Intercessors are often called "gapers" (Ezekiel 13:5, 22:30).

God looked for a man to stand in the gap and He found none. (Isaiah 58:12) talks about repairing the breach, it is important to understand how to stand in the gap and to repair.

Gap means that there is a tear or a breaking in the wall. Gap means to break forth or break down. Because of the Gap between God and man, intercessors try to repair and close the gap for the people of God. The intercessor always come to God on behalf of man. The Lord is seeking for a man (nor gender based).

There is a two-fold responsibility for the intercessor:

Make a wall for a hedge around the people.

Stand in the gap (plug in the breach)

Intercessors link God's mercy to the human need. When a wall was torn down, in order to keep intruders from coming in, there had to be people standing to cover the section where there was a breach.

Notes

THE PRAYER LIFE OF JESUS

Prayer should be important to us because it was important to the Lord Jesus. Jesus is our role model of intercessory prayer. Study each of the following references about the prayer life of Jesus:

He prayed any time of the day or night (Luke 6:12-13)

Prayer took priority overeating (John 4:31-32)

Prayer took priority over business (John 4:31-32)

He taught prayer to His disciples (Matthew 6:9-13)

Jesus made prayer a priority.

At his baptism (Luke 3:21-22)

During the first ministry tour (Mark 1:35; Luke 5:16)

Before the choice of the disciples (Luke 6:12-13)

Before/after feeding the 5,00 (Matt 14:19,23; Mark 6:41,46; John 6:11, 14 -15

At the feeding of the 4,000 (Matt 15:36; Mark 8:6-7)

Before the confession of Peter (Luke 9:18)

Before the transfiguration (Luke 9:28-29)

At the return of the seventy (Matt 19:13)

At the grace of Lazarus (John 11:41-42)

At the blessing of the children (Matt 19:13)

At the coming of certain Greeks (John 12:27-28

For Peter (Luke 22:32)

For the giving of the Holy Spirit (John 14:16)

On the road to Emmaus (Luke 24:30-31)

Prior to His ascension (Luke 24:50-53)

For His followers (John 17)

Before His great trial (Matt 26:26-27; Mark 14:22-23)

Notes

AUTHORITY AND POWER

And behold, I send the promise of my father upon you; but tarry ye in the city of Jerusalem until ye be endued with power from one high (Luke 24:49)

Like the policeman, you must have, both authority and power to be effective in intercession for you are actually doing spiritual battle with Satan. Believers receive authority through the new birth expe- rience and their position in Christ but some never go on to receive the power of the Holy Spirit that must be combined with authority to intercede effectively.

Satan has limited power but he has no authority. Jesus gave us both power and authority over all the power of the enemy. The power Jesus gave is directed power to be used for specific purposes in intercession:

Power of the Enemy

You have authority to intercede in prayer for those who need healing and deliverance:

Then He called His twelve disciples together and gave them power and authority over all devils, and to cure diseases (Luke 9:1)

Power Over Sin

You have authority to intercede for those who need salvation: Whosoever sins ye remit, they are remitted unto them; and whosoev-er sins ye retain, they are retained (John 20:22).

Power to Extend the Gospel

You have authority to pray for laborers to extend the Gospel:

Then He said to His disciples, "The harvest truly is plentiful, but the laborers are few. Therefore, pray the Lord of the harvest to send out laborers into His harvest." (Matthew 9:36-37)

Binding and Loosing

The term "to bind" originates from the Hebrew word asar, meaning, "to bind, imprison, tie, gird, to harness." The word occurs approximately 70 times in the Hebrew Old Testament and was often used to indicate the tying up of horses and donkeys (2Kings 7:10).

The remarks of Jesus in Matthew 12:28-29 are of great significance. But if I cast out demons by the Spirit of God, surely the kingdom of God has come upon you. Or else, how can one enter a strong man's house and plunder his goods unless he first binds the strong man? And then he will plunder his house.

It is impossible to take the possessions of the strong man without first of all binding the strong man. Jesus, in speaking of the strong man, is referring to Satan. Those possessions which are to be taken from him are his most prized possessions of all, lost individuals en- slaved by him, including those who are "demonized".

Jesus gave believers the power to bind and loose:

And I will give unto there the keys of the Kingdom of Heaven; and whatsoever thou shalt bind on earth shall be bound in Heaven; and whatever thou shalt loose on earth shall be loosed in Heaven (Matt.16:19).

Jesus taught the importance of binding evil spirits before casting them out, but the principle of binding and loosing extends to more than casting out demons. You can bind the power of the enemy to work in your life, home, community and church fellowship.

You can lose men and women from the bondage of sin, depression and discouragement of the enemy. In every situation, every problem, every challenge, there is a spiritual key. That key is binding and loosing through intercessory prayer.

Notes

Notes

A TEACHING ON WATCHES

There are 8 watches and they can be categorized as follows:

1st Watch: From 6pm to 9pm

To rest and release anxieties before the Lord; to read, pray and have quiet reflections. Receive clear directions from God and also prepares you for the next day, usually for those with a strong apostolic calling on their life. Seasoned Christians are usually the ones who are on this watch, those who are determined to do mighty things for the Lord (Matthew 14:15-23).

Covenant renewal with God. WE can also appropriate God's blessings. Whatever happens during the day is the time a large extent of what is happening during the night.

2nd Watch: From 9pm to 12 midnight

During this watch, the enemy gets ready to impact the spiritual realm, before the enemy goes to attack; you are going into intercept before the witches' hour.

Diabolical assignments are set in place by the enemy, pray for protection over our families, cities and nations.

Divine judgements, prayer and deliverance for the economy, educational, religious and political systems (Psalms 68:1).

3rd Watch: This watch is the breaking of the day watch from 12 midnight till 3am

This is the time that Peter denied Jesus 3 times.

It is a time of warfare and heavy spiritual activity (Psalms 91:5-6).

It is called the witches' hour; this is when most incantations and spells are cast and things are released against you.

Time of fighting against spiritual war and things that have been set against you, most vulnerable because you are sleeping during this time, nightmares also come during this time as well.

There are many spiritual attacks that come during this hour; they plan car crashes and violations over you as well.

4th Watch: From 3am to 6am

Praying for God's release; time for deliverance and resurrection power.

This is also time of supernatural encounters; it is the time when Jesus walked on the water (Exodus 12 and 14).

Set the atmosphere, people become disciplined in this prayer watch.

Time for all the enemy's plans to fail. Gaining territory and establishing prosperity, a time for decreeing and declaring as well.

5th Watch: From 6am to 9am

This is the time God strengthens the saints, we pray for healing in our body, relationships, family, ministry, government and econo- my.

To be equipped with the holy spirit for service.

6th Watch: From 9am to 12pm-noon

Time for harvest of God's promises. Watchman guard over the word of the Lord to be fulfilled, expect manifestation of God's promises in your life.

Pray for provision to do God's work, pray for crucified life.

Prayer for forgiveness, healing of relationships and for more.

7th Watch: From 12noon to 3pm

Midday is an hour of rest and time to seek the Lord, historically time of redemption.

This was the watch that Daniel always went home to pray.

On another time, when promises are released, foundations are to exercise God given dominion.

7th Watch: From 12noon to 3pm

This is the time of the light of day, letting your full light shine, praying for a full and vibrant life, not to be led into any traps or snare of the enemy (Psa.91:1,5; Prov. 4:18)

Pray against temptations, snares and cut all satanic arrows.

8th Watch: From 3pm to 6pm

The hour of power and triumphant glory, a time of removing limiting.

The hour of revelation and grace.

The hour of the voice of the Lord, the time when Christ died.

The time to die to the world and to self.

Time to change shape or history as well.

Time for changing history as Christ changed history during this hour as well.

Notes

REFERENCES AND SCRIPTURES

Abraham Calling Upon the Name of The Lord

Genesis 12 KJV

Now the Lord had said unto Abram, get thee out of thy country, and from thy kindred, and from thy father's house, unto a land that I will shew thee:

2 And I will make of thee a great nation, and I will bless thee, and make thy name great; and thou shalt be a blessing:

3 And I will bless them that bless thee and curse him that curseth thee: and in thee shall all families of the earth be blessed.

4 So Abram departed, as the Lord had spoken unto him; and Lot went with him: and Abram was seventy and five years old when he departed out of Haran.

5 And Abram took Sarai his wife, and Lot his brother's son, and all their substance that they had gathered, and the souls that they had gotten in Haran; and they went forth to go into the land of Canaan; and into the land of Canaan, they came.

6 And Abram passed through the land unto the place of Sichem, unto the plain of Moreh. And the Canaanite was then in the land.

7 And the Lord appeared unto Abram, and said, unto thy seed will I give this land: and there builded he an altar unto the Lord, who appeared unto him.

8 And he removed from thence unto a mountain on the east of Bethel, and pitched his tent, having Bethel on the west, and Hai on the east: and there he builded an altar unto the Lord, and called upon the name of the Lord.

9 And Abram journeyed, going on still toward the south.

10 And there was a famine in the land: and Abram went down into Egypt to sojourn there; for the famine was grievous in the land.

11 And it came to pass, when he was come near to enter into Egypt, that he said unto Sarai his wife, behold now, I know that thou art a fair woman to look upon:

12 Therefore it shall come to pass, when the Egyptians shall see thee, that they

shall say, this is his wife: and they will kill me, but they will save thee alive.

¹³ Say, I pray thee, thou art my sister: that it may be well with me for thy sake; and my soul shall live because of thee.

¹⁴ And it came to pass, that, when Abram was come into Egypt, the Egyptians beheld the woman that she was very fair.

¹⁵ The princes also of Pharaoh saw her and commended her before Pharaoh: and the woman was taken into Pharaoh's house.

¹⁶ And he entreated Abram well for her sake: and he had sheep, and oxen, and he asses, and menservants, and maidservants, and she asses, and camels.

¹⁷ And the Lord plagued Pharaoh and his house with great plagues because of Sarai Abram's wife.

¹⁸ And Pharaoh called Abram and said, what is this that thou hast done unto me? why didst thou not tell me that she was thy wife?

¹⁹ Why saidst thou, she is my sister? so I might have taken her to me to wife: now therefore behold thy wife, take her, and go thy way.

²⁰ And Pharaoh commanded his men concerning him: and they sent him away, and his wife, and all that he had.

Crying unto God

Psalms 27 KJV

The Lord is my light and my salvation; whom shall I fear? the Lord is the strength of my life; of whom shall I be afraid?

² When the wicked, even mine enemies and my foes, came upon me to eat up my flesh, they stumbled and fell.

3 Though an host should encamp against me, my heart shall not fear: though war should rise against me, in this will I be confident.

⁴ One thing have I desired of the Lord, that will I seek after; that I may dwell in the house of the Lord all the days of my life, to behold the beauty of the Lord, and to enquire in his temple.

⁵ For in the time of trouble he shall hide me in his pavilion: in the secret of his tabernacle shall he hide me; he shall set me up upon a rock.

⁶ And now shall mine head be lifted up above mine enemies round about me: therefore, will I offer in his tabernacle sacrifices of joy; I will sing, yea, I will sing praises unto the Lord.

⁷ Hear, O Lord, when I cry with my voice: have mercy also upon me and answer me.

⁸ When thou saidst, seek ye my face; my heart said unto thee, Thy face, Lord, will I seek.

⁹ Hide not thy face far from me; put not thy servant away in anger: thou hast been my help; leave me not, neither forsake me, O God of my salvation.

¹⁰ When my father and my mother forsake me, then the Lord will take me up.

¹¹ Teach me thy way, O Lord, and lead me in a plain path, because of mine enemies.

¹² Deliver me not over unto the will of mine enemies: for false witnesses are risen up against me, and such as breathe out cruelty.

¹³ I had fainted unless I had believed to see the goodness of the Lord in the land of the living.

¹⁴ Wait on the Lord: be of good courage, and he shall strengthen thine heart: wait, I say, on the Lord.

Drawing near to God

Psalms 73 KJV

Truly God is good to Israel, even to such as are of a clean heart.

² But as for me, my feet were almost gone; my steps had well-nigh slipped.

³ For I was envious at the foolish, when I saw the prosperity of the wicked.

⁴ For there are no bands in their death: but their strength is firm.

⁵ They are not in trouble as other men; neither are they plagued like other men.

⁶ Therefore pride compasseth them about as a chain; violence covereth them as a garment.

7 Their eyes stand out with fatness: they have more than heart could wish.

8 They are corrupt and speak wickedly concerning oppression: they speak loftily.

9 They set their mouth against the heavens, and their tongue walketh through the earth.

10 Therefore his people return hither: and waters of a full cup are wrung out to them.

11 And they say, how doth God know? and is there knowledge in the most High?

11 And they say, how doth God know? and is there knowledge in the most High?

12 Behold, these are the ungodly, who prosper in the world; they increase in riches.

13 Verily I have cleansed my heart in vain and washed my hands in innocence.

14 For all day long have I been plagued and chastened every morning.

15 If I say, I will speak; thus, behold, I should offend against the generation of thy children.

16 When I thought to know this, it was too painful for me.

17 Until I went into the sanctuary of God; then understood I their end.

18 Surely, thou didst set them in slippery places: thou castedst them down into destruction.

19 How are they brought into desolation, as in a moment! They are utterly consumed with terrors.

20 As a dream when one awaketh; so, O Lord, when thou awakest, thou shalt despise their image.

21 Thus my heart was grieved, and I was pricked in my reins.

22 So foolish was I, and ignorant: I was as a beast before thee.

23 Nevertheless I am continually with thee: thou hast holden me by my right hand.

²⁴ Thou shalt guide me with thy counsel, and afterward receive me to glory.

²⁵ Whom have I in heaven but thee? and there is none upon earth that I desire beside thee.

²⁶ My flesh and my heart faileth: but God is the strength of my heart, and my portion forever.

²⁷ For, lo, they that are far from thee shall perish: thou hast destroyed all them that go a whoring from thee.

²⁸ But it is good for me to draw near to God: I have put my trust in the Lord God, that I may declare all thy works.

Hebrews 10 KJV

For the law having a shadow of good things to come, and not the very image of the things, can never with those sacrifices which they offered year by year continually make the comers thereunto perfect.

² For then would they not have ceased to be offered? because that the worshippers once purged should have had no more conscience of sins.

³ But in those sacrifices, there is a remembrance again made of sins every year.

4 For it is not possible that the blood of bulls and of goats should take away sins.

⁵ Wherefore when he cometh into the world, he saith, Sacrifice and offering thou wouldest not, but a body hast thou prepared me:

⁶ In burnt offerings and sacrifices for sin thou hast had no pleasure.

⁷ Then said I, Lo, I come (in the volume of the book it is written of me,) to do thy will, O God.

⁸ Above when he said, Sacrifice and offering and burnt offerings and offering for sin thou wouldest not, neither hadst pleasure therein; which are offered by the law; ⁹ Then said he, Lo, I come to do thy will, O God. He taketh away the first, that he may establish the second.

¹⁰ By the which will we are sanctified through the offering of the body of Jesus Christ once for all.

¹¹ And every priest standeth daily ministering and offering oftentimes the same sacrifices, which can never take away sins:

¹² But this man, after he had offered one sacrifice for sins forever, sat down on the right hand of God.

¹³ From henceforth expecting till his enemies be made his footstool.

¹⁴ For by one offering he hath perfected forever them that are sanctified.

¹⁵ Whereof the Holy Ghost also is a witness to us: for after that he had said before,

¹⁶ This is the covenant that I will make with them after those days, saith the Lord, I will put my laws into their hearts, and in their minds will I write them.

¹⁷ And their sins and iniquities will I remember no more.

¹⁸ Now where remission of these is, there is no more offering for sin.

¹⁹ Having therefore, brethren, boldness to enter into the holiest by the blood of Jesus,

²⁰ By a new and living way, which he hath consecrated for us, through the veil, that is to say, his flesh.

²¹ And having an high priest over the house of God;

²² Let us draw near with a true heart in full assurance of faith, having our hearts sprinkled from an evil conscience, and our bodies washed with pure water.

²³ Let us hold fast the profession of our faith without wavering; (for he is faithful that promised;)

²⁴ And let us consider one another to provoke unto love and to good works:

²⁵ Not forsaking the assembling of ourselves together, as the manner of some is; but exhorting one another: and so much the more, as ye see the day approaching.

²⁶ For if we sin wilfully after that we have received the knowledge of the truth, there remaineth no more sacrifice for sins,

27 But a certain fearful looking for of judgment and fiery indignation, which shall devour the adversaries.

28 He that despised Moses' law died without mercy under two or three witnesses:

29 Of how much sorer punishment, suppose ye, shall he be thought worthy, who hath trodden underfoot the Son of God, and hath counted the blood of the covenant, wherewith he was sanctified, an unholy thing, and hath done despite unto the Spirit of grace?

Looking Up

Psalms 5 KJV

Give ear to my words, O Lord, consider my meditation.

2 Hearken unto the voice of my cry, my King, and my God: for unto thee will I pray.

3 My voice shalt thou hear in the morning, O Lord; in the morning will I direct my prayer unto thee and will look up.

4 For thou art not a God that hath pleasure in wickedness: neither shall evil dwell with thee.

5 The foolish shall not stand in thy sight: thou hatest all workers of iniquity.

6 Thou shalt destroy them that speak leasing: the Lord will abhor the bloody and deceitful man.

7 But as for me, I will come into thy house in the multitude of thy mercy: and in thy fear will I worship toward thy holy temple.

Lifting up the Soul

Psalms 25 KJV

Unto thee, O Lord, do I lift up my soul.

2 O my God, I trust in thee: let me not be ashamed, let not mine enemies triumph over me.

3 Yea, let none that wait on thee be ashamed: let them be ashamed which

transgress without cause.

⁴Shew me thy ways, O Lord; teach me thy paths.

⁵ Lead me in thy truth and teach me: for thou art the God of my salvation; on thee do I wait all the day.

⁶Remember, O Lord, thy tender mercies, and thy loving kindnesses; for they have been ever of old.

⁷ Remember not the sins of my youth, nor my transgressions: according to thy mercy remember thou me for thy goodness' sake, O Lord.

⁸Good and upright is the Lord: therefore, will he teach sinners in the way.

⁹The meek will he guide in judgment: and the meek will he teach his way.

¹⁰ All the paths of the Lord are mercy and truth unto such as keep his covenant and his testimonies.

¹¹For thy name's sake, O Lord, pardon mine iniquity; for it is great.

¹² What man is he that feareth the Lord? him shall he teach in the way that he shall choose.

¹³His soul shall dwell at ease; and his seed shall inherit the earth.

¹⁴ The secret of the Lord is with them that fear him; and he will shew them his covenant.

¹⁵ Mine eyes are ever toward the Lord; for he shall pluck my feet out of the net.

¹⁶ Turn thee unto me and have mercy upon me; for I am desolate and afflicted.

¹⁷ The troubles of my heart are enlarged: O bring thou me out of my distresses.

¹⁸ Look upon mine affliction and my pain; and forgive all my sins.

¹⁹ Consider mine enemies; for they are many; and they hate me with cruel hatred.

²⁰ O keep my soul, and deliver me: let me not be ashamed; for I put my trust in thee.

²¹ Let integrity and uprightness preserve me; for I wait on thee.

²² Redeem Israel, O God, out of all his troubles.

Lifting up the Heart

Lamentations 3:41KJV

⁴¹ Let us lift up our heart with our hands unto God in the heavens.

Pouring out the heart

Psalms 62 KJV

Truly my soul waiteth upon God: from him cometh my salvation.

² He only is my rock and my salvation; he is my defence; I shall not be greatly moved.

³ How long will ye imagine mischief against a man? ye shall be slain all of you: as a bowing wall shall ye be, and as a tottering fence.

⁴ They only consult to cast him down from his excellency: they delight in lies: they bless with their mouth, but they curse inwardly. Selah.

⁵ My soul, wait thou only upon God; for my expectation is from him.

⁶ He only is my rock and my salvation: he is my defence; I shall not be moved.

⁷ In God is my salvation and my glory: the rock of my strength, and my refuge, is in God.

⁸ Trust in him at all times; ye people, pour out your heart before him: God is a refuge for us. Selah.

⁹ Surely men of low degree are vanity, and men of high degree are a lie: to be laid in the balance, they are altogether lighter than vanity.

¹⁰ Trust not in oppression and become not vain in robbery: if riches increase, set not your heart upon them.

¹¹ God hath spoken once; twice have I heard this; that power belongeth unto God.

¹² Also unto thee, O Lord, belongeth mercy: for thou renderest to every man according to his work.

Pouring out the Soul

1Samuel 1 KJV

Now there was a certain man of Ramathaimzophim, of mount Ephraim, and his name was Elkanah, the son of Jeroham, the son of Elihu, the son of Tohu, the son of Zuph, an Ephrathite:

² And he had two wives; the name of the one was Hannah, and the name of the other Peninnah: and Peninnah had children, but Hannah had no children.

³ And this man went up out of his city yearly to worship and to sacrifice unto the Lord of hosts in Shiloh. And the two sons of Eli, Hophni and Phinehas, the priests of the Lord, were there.

⁴ And when the time was that Elkanah offered, he gave to Peninnah his wife, and to all her sons and her daughters, portions:

⁵ But unto Hannah he gave a worthy portion; for he loved Hannah: but the Lord had shut up her womb.

⁶ And her adversary also provoked her sore, for to make her fret, because the Lord had shut up her womb.

⁷ And as he did so year by year, when she went up to the house of the Lord, so she provoked her; therefore she wept, and did not eat.

⁸ Then said Elkanah her husband to her, Hannah, why weepest thou? and why eatest thou not? and why is thy heart grieved? am not I better to thee than ten sons?

⁹ So Hannah rose up after they had eaten in Shiloh, and after they had drunk. Now Eli the priest sat upon a seat by a post of the temple of the Lord.

¹⁰ And she was in bitterness of soul, and prayed unto the Lord, and wept sore.

¹³ Now Hannah, she spake in her heart; only her lips moved, but her voice was not heard: therefore Eli thought she had been drunken.

¹⁴ And Eli said unto her, how long wilt thou be drunken? put away thy wine from thee.

¹⁵ And Hannah answered and said, No, my lord, I am a woman of a sorrowful spirit: I have drunk neither wine nor strong drink, but have poured

out my soul before the Lord.

¹⁶ Count not thine handmaid for a daughter of Belial: for out of the abundance of my complaint and grief have I spoken hitherto.

¹⁷ Then Eli answered and said, Go in peace: and the God of Israel grant thee thy petition that thou hast asked of him.

¹⁸ And she said, Let thine handmaid find grace in thy sight. So the woman went her way, and did eat, and her countenance was no more sad.

¹⁹ And they rose up in the morning early, and worshipped before the Lord, and returned, and came to their house to Ramah: and Elkanah knew Hannah his wife; and the Lord remembered her.

²⁰ Wherefore it came to pass, when the time was come about after Hannah had conceived, that she bare a son, and called his name Samuel, saying, Because I have asked him of the Lord.

²¹ And the man Elkanah, and all his house, went up to offer unto the Lord the yearly sacrifice, and his vow.

²² But Hannah went not up; for she said unto her husband, I will not go up until the child be weaned, and then I will bring him, that he may appear before the Lord, and there abide for ever.

²³ And Elkanah her husband said unto her, Do what seemeth thee good; tarry until thou have weaned him; only the Lord establish his word. So the woman abode, and gave her son suck until she weaned him.

²⁴ And when she had weaned him, she took him up with her, with three bullocks, and one ephah of flour, and a bottle of wine, and brought him unto the house of the Lord in Shiloh: and the child was young.

²⁵ And they slew a bullock, and brought the child to Eli.

²⁶ And she said, Oh my lord, as thy soul liveth, my lord, I am the woman that stood by thee here, praying unto the Lord.

²⁷ For this child I prayed; and the Lord hath given me my petition which I asked of him:

²⁸ Therefore also I have lent him to the Lord; as long as he liveth he shall be

lent to the Lord. And he worshipped the Lord there.

Crying to Heaven

2 Chronicles 32 KJV

After these things, and the establishment thereof, Sennacherib king of Assyria came, and entered into Judah, and encamped against the fenced cities, and thought to win them for himself.

[2] And when Hezekiah saw that Sennacherib was come, and that he was purposed to fight against Jerusalem,

[3] He took counsel with his princes and his mighty men to stop the waters of the fountains which were without the city: and they did help him.

[4] So there was gathered much people together, who stopped all the fountains, and the brook that ran through the midst of the land, saying, Why should the kings of Assyria come, and find much water?

[5] Also he strengthened himself, and built up all the wall that was broken, and raised it up to the towers, and another wall without, and repaired Millo in the city of David, and made darts and shields in abundance.

[6] And he set captains of war over the people, and gathered them together to him in the street of the gate of the city, and spake comfortably to them, saying,

[7] Be strong and courageous, be not afraid nor dismayed for the king of Assyria, nor for all the multitude that is with him: for there be more with us than with him:

[8] With him is an arm of flesh; but with us is the Lord our God to help us, and to fight our battles. And the people rested themselves upon the words of Hezekiah king of Judah.

[9] After this did Sennacherib king of Assyria send his servants to Jerusalem, (but he himself laid siege against Lachish, and all his power with him,) unto Hezekiah king of Judah, and unto all Judah that were at Jerusalem, saying,

[10] Thus saith Sennacherib king of Assyria, Whereon do ye trust, that ye abide in the siege in Jerusalem?

[11] Doth not Hezekiah persuade you to give over yourselves to die by famine

and by thirst, saying, The Lord our God shall deliver us out of the hand of the king of Assyria?

[12] commanded Hath not the same Hezekiah taken away his high places and his altars, and Judah and Jerusalem, saying, Ye shall worship before one altar, and burn incense upon it?

[13] Know ye not what I and my fathers have done unto all the people of other lands? were the gods of the nations of those lands any ways able to deliver their lands out of mine hand?

[14] Who was there among all the gods of those nations that my fathers utterly destroyed, that could deliver his people out of mine hand, that your God should be able to deliver you out of mine hand?

[15] Now therefore let not Hezekiah deceive you, nor persuade you on this manner, neither yet believe him: for no god of any nation or kingdom was able to deliver his people out of mine hand, and out of the hand of my fathers: how much less shall your God deliver you out of mine hand?

[16] And his servants spake yet more against the Lord God, and against his servant Hezekiah.

[17] He wrote also letters to rail on the Lord God of Israel, and to speak against him, saying, As the gods of the nations of other lands have not delivered their people out of mine hand, so shall not the God of Hezekiah deliver his people out of mine hand.

[18] Then they cried with a loud voice in the Jews' speech unto the people of Jerusalem that were on the wall, to affright them, and to trouble them; that they might take the city.

[19] And they spake against the God of Jerusalem, as against the gods of the people of the earth, which were the work of the hands of man.

[20] And for this cause Hezekiah the king, and the prophet Isaiah the son of Amoz, pr

[21] And the Lord sent an angel, which cut off all the mighty men of valour, and the leaders and captains in the camp of the king of Assyria. So he returned

with shame of face to his own land. And when he was come into the house of his god, they that came forth of his own bowels slew him there with the sword.

²² Thus the Lord saved Hezekiah and the inhabitants of Jerusalem from the hand of Sennacherib the king of Assyria, and from the hand of all other, and guided them on every side.

²³ And many brought gifts unto the Lord to Jerusalem, and presents to Hezekiah king of Judah: so that he was magnified in the sight of all nations from thenceforth.

²⁴ In those days Hezekiah was sick to the death, and prayed unto the Lord: and he spake unto him, and he gave him a sign.

²⁵ But Hezekiah rendered not again according to the benefit done unto him; for his heart was lifted up: therefore there was wrath upon him, and upon Judah and Jerusalem.

²⁶ Notwithstanding Hezekiah humbled himself for the pride of his heart, both he and the inhabitants of Jerusalem, so that the wrath of the Lord came not upon them in the days of Hezekiah.

²⁷ And Hezekiah had exceeding much riches and honour: and he made himself treasuries for silver, and for gold, and for precious stones, and for spices, and for shields, and for all manner of pleasant jewels;

²⁸ Storehouses also for the increase of corn, and wine, and oil; and stalls for all manner of beasts, and cotes for flocks.

²⁹ Moreover he provided him cities, and possessions of flocks and herds in abundance: for God had given him substance very much.

³⁰ This same Hezekiah also stopped the upper watercourse of Gihon, and brought it straight down to the west side of the city of David. And Hezekiah prospered in all his works.

³¹ Howbeit in the business of the ambassadors of the princes of Babylon, who sent unto him to enquire of the wonder that was done in the land, God left him, to try him, that he might know all that was in his heart.

³² Now the rest of the acts of Hezekiah, and his goodness, behold, they are

written in the vision of Isaiah the prophet, the son of Amoz, and in the book of the kings of Judah and Israel.

33 And Hezekiah slept with his fathers, and they buried him in the chiefest of the sepulchres of the sons of David: and all Judah and the inhabitants of Jerusalem did him honour at his death. And Manasseh his son reigned in his stead.

Beseeching the Lord

Exodus 32 KJV

And when the people saw that Moses delayed coming down out of the mount, the people gathered themselves together unto Aaron, and said unto him, Up, make us gods, which shall go before us; for as for this Moses, the man that brought us up out of the land of Egypt, we wot not what is become of him.

2 And Aaron said unto them, break off the golden earrings, which are in the ears of your wives, of your sons, and of your daughters, and bring them unto me.

3 And all the people brake off the golden earrings which were in their ears, and brought them unto Aaron.

4 And he received them at their hand, and fashioned it with a graving tool, after he had made it a molten calf: and they said, These be thy gods, O Israel, which brought thee up out of the land of Egypt.

5 And when Aaron saw it, he built an altar before it; and Aaron made proclamation, and said, Tomorrow is a feast to the Lord.

6 And they rose up early on the morrow, and offered burnt offerings, and brought peace offerings; and the people sat down to eat and to drink, and rose up to play.

7 And the Lord said unto Moses, Go, get thee down; for thy people, which thou broughtest out of the land of Egypt, have corrupted themselves:

8 They have turned aside quickly out of the way which I commanded them: they have made them a molten calf, and have worshipped it, and have

sacrificed thereunto, and said, These be thy gods, O Israel, which have brought thee up out of the land of Egypt.

⁹ And the Lord said unto Moses, I have seen this people, and, behold, it is a stiffnecked people:

¹⁰ Now therefore let me alone, that my wrath may wax hot against them, and that I may consume them: and I will make of thee a great nation.

¹¹ And Moses besought the Lord his God, and said, Lord, why doth thy wrath wax hot against thy people, which thou hast brought forth out of the land of Egypt with great power, and with a mighty hand?

¹² Wherefore should the Egyptians speak, and say, For mischief did he bring them out, to slay them in the mountains, and to consume them from the face of the earth? Turn from thy fierce wrath, and repent of this evil against thy people.

¹³ Remember Abraham, Isaac, and Israel, thy servants, to whom thou swarest by thine own self, and saidst unto them, I will multiply your seed as the stars of heaven, and all this land that I have spoken of will I give unto your seed, and they shall inherit it forever.

¹⁴ And the Lord repented of the evil which he thought to do unto his people.

¹⁵ And Moses turned, and went down from the mount, and the two tables of the testimony were in his hand: the tables were written on both their sides; on the one side and on the other were they written.

¹⁶ And the tables were the work of God, and the writing was the writing of God, graven upon the tables.

¹⁷ And when Joshua heard the noise of the people as they shouted, he said unto Moses, There is a noise of war in the camp.

¹⁸ And he said, It is not the voice of them that shout for mastery, neither is it the voice of them that cry for being overcome: but the noise of them that sing do I hear.

¹⁹ And it came to pass, as soon as he came nigh unto the camp, that he saw the calf, and the dancing: and Moses' anger waxed hot, and he cast the tables out

of his hands, and brake them beneath the mount.

²⁰ And he took the calf which they had made, and burnt it in the fire, and ground it to powder, and strawed it upon the water, and made the children of Israel drink of it.

²¹ And Moses said unto Aaron, What did this people unto thee, that thou hast brought so great a sin upon them?

²² And Aaron said, Let not the anger of my lord wax hot: thou knowest the people, that they are set on mischief.

²³ For they said unto me, Make us gods, which shall go before us: for as for this Moses, the man that brought us up out of the land of Egypt, we wot not what is become of him.

²⁴ And I said unto them, whosoever hath any gold, let them break it off. So they gave it me: then I cast it into the fire, and there came out this calf.

²⁵ And when Moses saw that the people were naked; (for Aaron had made them naked unto their shame among their enemies:)

²⁶ Then Moses stood in the gate of the camp, and said, Who is on the Lord's side? let him come unto me. And all the sons of Levi gathered themselves together unto him. ²⁷ And he said unto them, Thus saith the Lord God of Israel, Put every man his sword by his side, and go in and out from gate to gate throughout the camp, and slay every man his brother, and every man his companion, and every man his neighbour.

²⁸ And the children of Levi did according to the word of Moses: and there fell of the people that day about three thousand men.

²⁹ For Moses had said, consecrate yourselves today to the Lord, even every man upon his son, and upon his brother; that he may bestow upon you a blessing this day.

³⁰ And it came to pass on the morrow, that Moses said unto the people, Ye have sinned a great sin: and now I will go up unto the Lord; peradventure I shall make an atonement for your sin.

³¹ And Moses returned unto the Lord, and said, Oh, this people have sinned

a great sin, and have made them gods of gold.

³² Yet now, if thou wilt forgive their sin--; and if not, blot me, I pray thee, out of thy book which thou hast written.

³³ And the Lord said unto Moses, Whosoever hath sinned against me, him will I blot out of my book.

³⁴ Therefore now go, lead the people unto the place of which I have spoken unto thee: behold, mine Angel shall go before thee: nevertheless in the day when I visit I will visit their sin upon them.

³⁵ And the Lord plagued the people, because they made the calf, which Aaron made.

Standing

Chronicles 20 KJV

It came to pass after this also, that the children of Moab, and the children of Ammon, and with them other beside the Ammonites, came against Jehoshaphat to battle.

² Then there came some that told Jehoshaphat, saying, There cometh a great multitude against thee from beyond the sea on this side Syria; and, behold, they be in Hazazontamar, which is Engedi.

And Jehoshaphat feared, and set himself to seek the Lord, and proclaimed a fast throughout all Judah.

⁴ And Judah gathered themselves together, to ask help of the Lord: even out of all the cities of Judah they came to seek the Lord.

⁵ And Jehoshaphat stood in the congregation of Judah and Jerusalem, in the house of the Lord, before the new court,

⁶ And said, O Lord God of our fathers, art not thou God in heaven? and rulest not thou over all the kingdoms of the heathen? and in thine hand is there not power and might, so that none is able to withstand thee?

⁷ Art not thou our God, who didst drive out the inhabitants of this land before thy people Israel, and gavest it to the seed of Abraham thy friend for ever?

⁸ And they dwelt therein, and have built thee a sanctuary therein for thy name, saying,

⁹ If, when evil cometh upon us, as the sword, judgment, or pestilence, or famine, we stand before this house, and in thy presence, (for thy name is in this house,) and cry unto thee in our affliction, then thou wilt hear and help.

¹⁰ And now, behold, the children of Ammon and Moab and mount Seir, whom thou wouldest not let Israel invade, when they came out of the land of Egypt, but they turned from them, and destroyed them not;

¹¹ Behold, I say, how they reward us, to come to cast us out of thy possession, which thou hast given us to inherit.

¹² O our God, wilt thou not judge them? for we have no might against this great company that cometh against us; neither know we what to do: but our eyes are upon thee.

¹³ And all Judah stood before the Lord, with their little ones, their wives, and their children.

¹⁴ Then upon Jahaziel the son of Zechariah, the son of Benaiah, the son of Jeiel, the son of Mattaniah, a Levite of the sons of Asaph, came the Spirit of the Lord in the midst of the congregation;

¹⁵ And he said, Hearken ye, all Judah, and ye inhabitants of Jerusalem, and thou king Jehoshaphat, Thus saith the Lord unto you, Be not afraid nor dismayed by reason of this great multitude; for the battle is not yours, but God's.

¹⁶ To morrow go ye down against them: behold, they come up by the cliff of Ziz; and ye shall find them at the end of the brook, before the wilderness of Jeruel.

¹⁷ Ye shall not need to fight in this battle: set yourselves, stand ye still, and see the salvation of the Lord with you, O Judah and Jerusalem: fear not, nor be dismayed; to morrow go out against them: for the Lord will be with you.

[18] And Jehoshaphat bowed his head with his face to the ground: and all Judah and the inhabitants of Jerusalem fell before the Lord, worshipping the Lord.

[19] And the Levites, of the children of the Kohathites, and of the children of the Korhites, stood up to praise the Lord God of Israel with a loud voice on high.

[20] And they rose early in the morning, and went forth into the wilderness of Tekoa: and as they went forth, Jehoshaphat stood and said, Hear me, O Judah, and ye inhabitants of Jerusalem; Believe in the Lord your God, so shall ye be established; believe his prophets, so shall ye prosper.

[21] And when he had consulted with the people, he appointed singers unto the Lord, and that should praise the beauty of holiness, as they went out before the army, and to say, Praise the Lord; for his mercy endureth for ever.

[22] And when they began to sing and to praise, the Lord set ambushments against the children of Ammon, Moab, and mount Seir, which were come against Judah; and they were smitten.

[23] For the children of Ammon and Moab stood up against the inhabitants of mount Seir, utterly to slay and destroy them: and when they had made an end of the inhabitants of Seir, every one helped to destroy another.

[24] And when Judah came toward the watch tower in the wilderness, they looked unto the multitude, and, behold, they were dead bodies fallen to the earth, and none escaped.

[25] And when Jehoshaphat and his people came to take away the spoil of them, they found among them in abundance both riches with the dead bodies, and precious jewels, which they stripped off for themselves, more than they could carry away: and they were three days in gathering of the spoil, it was so much.

[26] And on the fourth day they assembled themselves in the valley of Berachah; for there they blessed the Lord: therefore the name of the same place was called, The valley of Berachah, unto this day.

[27] Then they returned, every man of Judah and Jerusalem, and Jehoshaphat in the forefront of them, to go again to Jerusalem with joy; for the Lord had made them to rejoice over their enemies.

28 And they came to Jerusalem with psalteries and harps and trumpets unto the house of the Lord.

29 And the fear of God was on all the kingdoms of those countries, when they had heard that the Lord fought against the enemies of Israel.

30 So the realm of Jehoshaphat was quiet: for his God gave him rest round about.

31 And Jehoshaphat reigned over Judah: he was thirty and five years old when he began to reign, and he reigned twenty and five years in Jerusalem. And his mother's name was Azubah the daughter of Shilhi.

32 And he walked in the way of Asa his father, and departed not from it, doing that which was right in the sight of the Lord.

33 Howbeit the high places were not taken away: for as yet the people had not prepared their hearts unto the God of their fathers.

34 Now the rest of the acts of Jehoshaphat, first and last, behold, they are written in the book of Jehu the son of Hanani, who is mentioned in the book of the kings of Israel.

35 And after this did Jehoshaphat king of Judah join himself with Ahaziah king of Israel, who did very wickedly:

36 And he joined himself with him to make ships to go to Tarshish: and they made the ships in Eziongaber.

37 Then Eliezer the son of Dodavah of Mareshah prophesied against Jehoshaphat, saying, Because thou hast joined thyself with Ahaziah, the Lord hath broken thy works. And the ships were broken, that they were not able to go to Tarshish.

Daniel was Praying on his Knees.

Daniel 6 KJV

It pleased Darius to set over the kingdom an hundred and twenty princes, which should be over the whole kingdom;

2 And over these three presidents; of whom Daniel was first: that the princes

might give accounts unto them, and the king should have no damage.

³ Then this Daniel was preferred above the presidents and princes, because an excellent spirit was in him; and the king thought to set him over the whole realm.

⁴ Then the presidents and princes sought to find occasion against Daniel concerning the kingdom; but they could find no occasion nor fault; forasmuch as he was faithful, neither was there any error or fault found in him.

⁵ Then said these men, we shall not find any occasion against this Daniel, except we find it against him concerning the law of his God.

⁶ Then these presidents and princes assembled together to the king, and said thus unto him, King Darius, live forever.

⁷ All the presidents of the kingdom, the governors, and the princes, the counsellors, and the captains, have consulted together to establish a royal statute, and to make a firm decree, that whosoever shall ask a petition of any God or man for thirty days, save of thee, O king, he shall be cast into the den of lions.

⁸ Now, O king, establish the decree, and sign the writing, that it be not changed, according to the law of the Medes and Persians, which altereth not.

⁹ Wherefore king Darius signed the writing and the decree.

¹⁰ Now when Daniel knew that the writing was signed, he went into his house; and his windows being open in his chamber toward Jerusalem, he kneeled upon his knees three times a day, and prayed, and gave thanks before his God, as he did aforetime.

¹¹ Then these men assembled and found Daniel praying and making supplication before his God.

¹² Then they came near, and spake before the king concerning the king's decree; Hast thou not signed a decree, that every man that shall ask a petition of any God or man within thirty days, save of thee, O king, shall be cast into the den of lions? The king answered and said, The thing is true, according to the law of the Medes and Persians, which altereth not.

¹³ Then answered they and said before the king, That Daniel, which is of the

children of the captivity of Judah, regardeth not thee, O king, nor the decree that thou hast signed, but maketh his petition three times a day.

14 Then the king, when he heard these words, was sore displeased with himself, and set his heart on Daniel to deliver him: and he laboured till the going down of the sun to deliver him.

15 Then these men assembled unto the king, and said unto the king, Know, O king, that the law of the Medes and Persians is, That no decree nor statute which the king establisheth may be changed.

16 Then the king commanded, and they brought Daniel, and cast him into the den of lions. Now the king spake and said unto Daniel, Thy God whom thou servest continually, he will deliver thee.

17 And a stone was brought and laid upon the mouth of the den; and the king sealed it with his own signet, and with the signet of his lords; that the purpose might not be changed concerning Daniel.

18 Then the king went to his palace and passed the night fasting: neither were instruments of musick brought before him: and his sleep went from him.

19 Then the king arose very early in the morning and went in haste unto the den of lions.

20 And when he came to the den, he cried with a lamentable voice unto Daniel: and the king spake and said to Daniel, O Daniel, servant of the living God, is thy God, whom thou servest continually, able to deliver thee from the lions?

21 Then said Daniel unto the king, O king, live forever.

22 My God hath sent his angel, and hath shut the lions' mouths, that they have not hurt me: forasmuch as before him innocency was found in me; and also before thee, O king, have I done no hurt.

23 Then was the king exceedingly glad for him and commanded that they should take Daniel out of the den. So, Daniel was taken up out of the den, and no manner of hurt was found upon him, because he believed in his God.

24 And the king commanded, and they brought those men which had

accused Daniel, and they cast them into the den of lions, them, their children, and their wives; and the lions had the mastery of them and brake all their bones in pieces or ever they came at the bottom of the den.

²⁵ Then king Darius wrote unto all people, nations, and languages, that dwell in all the earth; Peace be multiplied unto you.

²⁶ I make a decree, that in every dominion of my kingdom men tremble and fear before the God of Daniel: for he is the living God, and stedfast forever, and his kingdom that which shall not be destroyed, and his dominion shall be even unto the end.

²⁷ He delivereth and rescueth, and he worketh signs and wonders in heaven and in earth, who hath delivered Daniel from the power of the lions.

²⁸ So this Daniel prospered in the reign of Darius, and in the reign of Cyrus the Persian.e children of the captivity of Judah, regardeth not thee, O king, nor the decree that thou hast signed, but maketh his petition three times a day.

King Solomon, kneeling on his Knees with his Hands Spread up to Heaven.

1Kings 8 KJV

Then Solomon assembled the elders of Israel, and all the heads of the tribes, the chief of the fathers of the children of Israel, unto king Solomon in Jerusalem, that they might bring up the ark of the covenant of the Lord out of the city of David, which is Zion.

² And all the men of Israel assembled themselves unto king Solomon at the feast in the month Ethanim, which is the seventh month.

³ And all the elders of Israel came, and the priests took up the ark.

⁴ And they brought up the ark of the Lord, and the tabernacle of the congregation, and all the holy vessels that were in the tabernacle, even those did the priests and the Levites bring up.

⁵ And king Solomon, and all the congregation of Israel, that were assembled unto him, were with him before the ark, sacrificing sheep and oxen, that could

not be told nor numbered for multitude.

⁶ And the priests brought in the ark of the covenant of the Lord unto his place, into the oracle of the house, to the most holy place, even under the wings of the cherubims.

⁷ For the cherubims spread forth their two wings over the place of the ark, and the cherubims covered the ark and the staves thereof above.

⁸ And they drew out the staves, that the ends of the staves were seen out in the holy place before the oracle, and they were not seen without: and there they are unto this day.

⁹ There was nothing in the ark save the two tables of stone, which Moses put there at Horeb, when the Lord made a covenant with the children of Israel, when they came out of the land of Egypt.

¹⁰ And it came to pass, when the priests were come out of the holy place, that the cloud filled the house of the Lord,

¹¹ So that the priests could not stand to minister because of the cloud: for the glory of the Lord had filled the house of the Lord.

¹² Then spake Solomon, The Lord said that he would dwell in the thick darkness.

¹³ I have surely built thee an house to dwell in, a settled place for thee to abide in for ever.

¹⁴ And the king turned his face about, and blessed all the congregation of Israel: (and all the congregation of Israel stood;)

¹⁵ And he said, Blessed be the Lord God of Israel, which spake with his mouth unto David my father, and hath with his hand fulfilled it, saying,

¹⁶ Since the day that I brought forth my people Israel out of Egypt, I chose no city out of all the tribes of Israel to build an house, that my name might be therein; but I chose David to be over my people Israel.

¹⁷ And it was in the heart of David my father to build an house for the name of the Lord God of Israel.

¹⁸ And the Lord said unto David my father, Whereas it was in thine heart to

build an house unto my name, thou didst well that it was in thine heart.

¹⁹ Nevertheless thou shalt not build the house; but thy son that shall come forth out of thy loins, he shall build the house unto my name.

²⁰ And the Lord hath performed his word that he spake, and I am risen up in the room of David my father, and sit on the throne of Israel, as the Lord promised, and have built an house for the name of the Lord God of Israel.

²¹ And I have set there a place for the ark, wherein is the covenant of the Lord, which he made with our fathers, when he brought them out of the land of Egypt. 22 And Solomon stood before the altar of the Lord in the presence of all the congregation of Israel, and spread forth his hands toward heaven:

²³ And he said, Lord God of Israel, there is no God like thee, in heaven above, or on earth beneath, who keepest covenant and mercy with thy servants that walk before thee with all their heart:

²⁴ Who hast kept with thy servant David my father that thou promisedst him: thou spakest also with thy mouth, and hast fulfilled it with thine hand, as it is this day. 25 Therefore now, Lord God of Israel, keep with thy servant David my father that thou promisedst him, saying, There shall not fail thee a man in my sight to sit on the throne of Israel; so that thy children take heed to their way, that they walk before me as thou hast walked before me.

²⁶ And now, O God of Israel, let thy word, I pray thee, be verified, which thou spakest unto thy servant David my father.

²⁷ But will God indeed dwell on the earth? behold, the heaven and heaven of heavens cannot contain thee; how much less this house that I have builded?

²⁸ Yet have thou respect unto the prayer of thy servant, and to his supplication, O Lord my God, to hearken unto the cry and to the prayer, which thy servant prayeth before thee to day:

²⁹ That thine eyes may be open toward this house night and day, even toward the place of which thou hast said, My name shall be there: that thou mayest hearken unto the prayer which thy servant shall make toward this place.

³⁰ And hearken thou to the supplication of thy servant, and of thy people

Israel, when they shall pray toward this place: and hear thou in heaven thy dwelling place: and when thou hearest, forgive.

31 If any man trespass against his neighbour, and an oath be laid upon him to cause him to swear, and the oath come before thine altar in this house:

32 Then hear thou in heaven, and do, and judge thy servants, condemning the wicked, to bring his way upon his head; and justifying the righteous, to give him according to his righteousness.

33 When thy people Israel be smitten down before the enemy, because they have sinned against thee, and shall turn again to thee, and confess thy name, and pray, and make supplication unto thee in this house:

34 Then hear thou in heaven, and forgive the sin of thy people Israel, and bring them again unto the land which thou gavest unto their fathers.

35 When heaven is shut up, and there is no rain, because they have sinned against thee; if they pray toward this place, and confess thy name, and turn from their sin, when thou afflictest them:

36 Then hear thou in heaven, and forgive the sin of thy servants, and of thy people Israel, that thou teach them the good way wherein they should walk, and give rain upon thy land, which thou hast given to thy people for an inheritance.

37 If there be in the land famine, if there be pestilence, blasting, mildew, locust, or if there be caterpiller; if their enemy besiege them in the land of their cities; whatsoever plague, whatsoever sickness there be;

38 What prayer and supplication soever be made by any man, or by all thy people Israel, which shall know every man the plague of his own heart, and spread forth his hands toward this house:

39 Then hear thou in heaven thy dwelling place, and forgive, and do, and give to every man according to his ways, whose heart thou knowest; (for thou, even thou only, knowest the hearts of all the children of men;)

40 That they may fear thee all the days that they live in the land which thou gavest unto our fathers.

[41] Moreover concerning a stranger, that is not of thy people Israel, but cometh out of a far country for thy name's sake.

[42] (For they shall hear of thy great name, and of thy strong hand, and of thy stretched-out arm;) when he shall come and pray toward this house;

[43] Hear thou in heaven thy dwelling place and do according to all that the stranger calleth to thee for: that all people of the earth may know thy name, to fear thee, as do thy people Israel; and that they may know that this house, which I have builded, is called by thy name.

[44] If thy people go out to battle against their enemy, whithersoever thou shalt send them, and shall pray unto the Lord toward the city which thou hast chosen, and toward the house that I have built for thy name:

[45] Then hear thou in heaven their prayer and their supplication and maintain their cause.

[46] If they sin against thee, (for there is no man that sinneth not,) and thou be angry with them, and deliver them to the enemy, so that they carry them away captives unto the land of the enemy, far or near;

[47] Yet if they shall bethink themselves in the land whither they were carried captives, and repent, and make supplication unto thee in the land of them that carried them captives, saying, We have sinned, and have done perversely, we have committed wickedness;

[48] And so return unto thee with all their heart, and with all their soul, in the land of their enemies, which led them away captive, and pray unto thee toward their land, which thou gavest unto their fathers, the city which thou hast chosen, and the house which I have built for thy name:

[49] Then hear thou their prayer and their supplication in heaven thy dwelling place, and maintain their cause,

[50] And forgive thy people that have sinned against thee, and all their transgressions wherein they have transgressed against thee, and give them compassion before them who carried them captive, that they may have compassion on them:

⁵¹ For they be thy people, and thine inheritance, which thou broughtest forth out of Egypt, from the midst of the furnace of iron:

⁵² That thine eyes may be open unto the supplication of thy servant, and unto the supplication of thy people Israel, to hearken unto them in all that they call for unto thee.

⁵³ For thou didst separate them from among all the people of the earth, to be thine inheritance, as thou spakest by the hand of Moses thy servant, when thou broughtest our fathers out of Egypt, O Lord God.

⁵⁴ And it was so, that when Solomon had made an end of praying all this prayer and supplication unto the Lord, he arose from before the altar of the Lord, from kneeling on his knees with his hands spread up to heaven.

⁵⁵ And he stood, and blessed all the congregation of Israel with a loud voice, saying,

⁵⁶ Blessed be the Lord, that hath given rest unto his people Israel, according to all that he promised: there hath not failed one word of all his good promise, which he promised by the hand of Moses his servant.

⁵⁷ The Lord our God be with us, as he was with our fathers: let him not leave us, nor forsake us:

⁵⁸ That he may incline our hearts unto him, to walk in all his ways, and to keep his commandments, and his statutes, and his judgments, which he commanded our fathers.

⁵⁹ And let these my words, wherewith I have made supplication before the Lord, be nigh unto the Lord our God Day and night, that he maintain the cause of his servant, and the cause of his people Israel at all times, as the matter shall require: ⁶⁰ That all the people of the earth may know that the Lord is God, and that there is none else.

⁶¹ Let your heart therefore be perfect with the Lord our God, to walk in his statutes, and to keep his commandments, as at this day.

⁶² And the king, and all Israel with him, offered sacrifice before the Lord.

⁶³ And Solomon offered a sacrifice of peace offerings, which he offered unto

the Lord, two and twenty thousand oxen, and an hundred and twenty thousand sheep. So the king and all the children of Israel dedicated the house of the Lord. [64] The same day did the king hallow the middle of the court that was before the house of the Lord: for there he offered burnt offerings, and meat offerings, and the fat of the peace offerings: because the brasen altar that was before the Lord was too little to receive the burnt offerings, and meat offerings, and the fat of the peace offerings.

[65] And at that time Solomon held a feast, and all Israel with him, a great congregation, from the entering in of Hamath unto the river of Egypt, before the Lord our God, seven days and seven days, even fourteen days.

[66] On the eighth day he sent the people away: and they blessed the king and went unto their tents joyful and glad of heart for all the goodness that the Lord had done for David his servant, and for Israel his people.

APOSTLE DR. DWAN JACKSON

She was born in Rochester, New York. She is a daughter of Mr. Bobby Lee Cox and Mrs. Dawn (Edward) G. Lewis. At the age of 5 she gave her life to Christ.

She is also a sister, a wife to Dr. Alfred Jackson and a mother of three.

Dr. Dwan Jackson received her bachelor's degree in Non-profit Ministry and Biblical studies from Ohio Christian University, and a Doctoral degree in Philosophy of Religious Studies from the Great Achievers International School of Theology, Valencia, Spain. In 1996 she founded Women of Virtue Ministries in Rochester, NY.

She was ordained, as an evangelist under Charles B. McCloud at Mt Carmel Deliverance Center in Rochester NY. As an evangelist, she ventured out and did street meetings and revivals. Dr. Jackson was ordained, as a pastor by Dr. Dr. Lloyd Benson Sr. She was also affirmed by a presbytery of Dr.s to the office of Dr. in 2008. She was also given credentials by the World link of churches and ministries better known as WLCM.

She travels extensively across the United States and has ventured overseas in countries such as South Africa, London, Canada, Jamaica, Ghana, Nigeria, Spain and the Bahamas amongst others spreading the Gospel of Jesus Christ. She is the founder of Women of Virtue International Ministries, Fresh Manna International Ministries and School of Ministries as well as the Senior **Leader of Pra**yer and Faith International Ministries.

FOR MORE INFORMATION

CORRESPONDENCE
Write to:
P.O. BOX 91022
Mobile, AL 36691
SOCIAL MEDIA
YouTube Channel Apostle Dr. Dwan Jackson
Instagram@jacksondwan

WEBSITE AND EMAIL ADDRESS
drdwanjacksonministries.org
dwanjackson44@gmail.com

www.ingramcontent.com/pod-product-compliance
Lightning Source LLC
Chambersburg PA
CBHW061717130726
47996CB00006B/2368